W9-AZB-626

Phoebe Eile

May 1966

A Treasury of Jewish Thoughts

A Treasury of Jewish Thoughts

edited by
Rabbi SAMUEL M. SILVER

illuminations by
EZEKIEL SCHLOSS

KTAV PUBLISHING HOUSE

47 Canal Street
New York, New York 10002

Library of Congress
Catalog Card Number: 64-16660

Wisdom is more precious than rubies . . .

Proverbs

JUDAISM teaches us that the path to true satisfaction is knowledge. To relay some of the wisdom in Judaism is the aim of this modest collection of Jewish sayings.

It is our hope that this collection will be truly enriching to all who read it.

May it also stimulate the reader to go further in the pursuit of wisdom and to make new discoveries in the wealth of Jewish lore.

TABLE OF CONTENTS

Bar Mitzvah

A boy at the age of thirteen assumes responsibility for the commandments.

Talmud

He who learns from another one chapter, one Halachah, one verse or one word or even a single letter is bound to respect him.

Pirke Avot

When ten people sit together and occupy themselves with Torah, the Shechinah (Divine Presence) abides among them.

Pirke Avot

Be not ashamed to learn and to seek knowledge; be a tail to the wise so that you may become a head.

Midrash

Brotherhood

You shall love your neighbor as yourself.

Bible

The non-Jew is your neighbor, your brother; to wrong him is to sin.

Midrash

Love therefore the stranger, for you were strangers in the land of Egypt.

Bible

If you have accustomed your tongue to speak evil of non-Jews, you will end by speaking evil of Israelites.

Midrash

Charity

He who is gracious unto the poor lendeth unto the Lord and his good deed will He repay him.

Bible

No one ever becomes impoverished by giving charity.

Maimonides

Charity knows neither race nor creed.

Talmud

If one can induce others to give, his reward is greater than the reward of the one who gives.

Shulhan Aruch

Death

The Lord gave, and the Lord has taken away; blessed be the name of the Lord.

Bible

The dust returns to the earth as it was, and the spirit returns to God who gave it.

Bible

Death is the means of transition to future life which is the ultimate goal of mortal existence.

Emunot Ve-Deot

The righteous are mightier in death than in life.

Talmud

Faith

The just shall live by his faith.
Bible

Few men endure patiently such misfortunes as poverty, sickness and terror. All these can be better endured with faith.

Solomon Ibn Gabirol

Even though He slay me yet will I trust in Him.

Bible

Faith is to do His will.

Apocrypha

Family Life

Honor your father and your mother.

Bible

"Your house is in peace" refers to one who loves his wife as himself and honors her more than himself, who leads his children in the right path.

Talmud

Rav Joseph, hearing the step of his mother, would say: I must stand up, for the Shechinah (Divine Presence) enters.

Talmud

The Bible considers the duty (of honoring parents) just as important as the duty of honoring and revering God.

Maimonides

Forgiveness

See mine affliction and my travail and forgive all my sins.

Bible

Forgive your neighbor his wrongdoing, then your sins will be forgiven when you pray.

Ben Sira

Open your heart to me (says God) as much as the thickness of a needle, and I will open it for you as wide as a portal.

Midrash

I will forgive their iniquity and their sin will I remember no more.

Bible

Friendship

There is that type of friend who clings closer than a brother.

Bible

Get yourself a companion, one to whom you can tell your secrets.

Pirke Avot

A friendless man is like a left hand bereft of the right.

Solomon Ibn Gabirol

It is easy to acquire an enemy, but difficult to acquire a friend.

Midrash

Honesty

He that works deceit shall not dwell within My House; He that speaks falsehood shall not be established before My eyes.

Bible

To be honest in business is to fulfill the entire Torah.

Midrash

Better is he who gives little to charity from money honestly earned than he who gives much from wealth gained through fraud.

Midrash

You shall not have weights of different sizes (to practice dishonesty).

Bible

Hospitality

Receive all men with a cheerful countenance.

Pirke Avot

The poor does for the host more than the host for the poor.

Midrash

He who receives a guest at his table ushers in the Shechinah (Divine Presence).

Talmud

Great is hospitality; greater even than early attendance at the house of study, or than the reception of the Holy Spirit.

Talmud

Humility

The humble shall inherit the land.

Bible

God loves nothing better than humility.

Midrash

Great is the man who ignores his own dignity and is not angered by affronts.

Midrash

Why was man created on the sixth day? To teach that if he is ever swollen with pride, it can be said to him: a flea came ahead of you in creation.

Talmud

Joy

Happy are those who dwell in Your house.

Bible

The Holy Spirit rests upon him only who has a joyous heart.

Talmud

A man will have to give account on the Judgment Day for every good thing which he might have enjoyed and did not.

Talmud

You shall rejoice before the Lord your God.

Bible

Justice

Justice, justice shall you pursue.
Bible

If there is no justice there is no peace.

Kad Ha-Kemah

Let justice well up as waters and righteousness as a mighty stream.

Bible

Execute true judgment and show mercy and compassion every man to his brother.

Bible

Kindness

Do not unto others what you do not wish others to do unto you.

Talmud

Let not kindness and truth forsake you.

Bible

Deeds of kindness are equal in weight to all the commandments.

Talmud

He who has a claim for money upon his neighbor and knows the latter is unable to pay, must not cross his path.

Talmud

Land of Israel

A land flowing with milk and honey.

Bible

The Land of Israel is the most beautiful of lands.

Midrash

The Lord said to Abraham: "Unto you and your seed will I give this land."

Bible

The Land of Israel is the holiest of lands.

Midrash

Learning

You shall study the Torah day and night.

Bible

Knowledge lifts the poor man's head and sets him among princes.

Ben Sira

A synagogue may be turned into a school.

Talmud

Just as a small burning tree may set a bigger tree on fire so may a young pupil sharpen the mind of a teacher and by means of questions stimulate him toward glorious wisdom.

Maimonides

Manners

Where there is no Torah, there are no manners, and without manners there is no Torah.

Pirke Avot

The test of good manners is to bear patiently with bad ones.

Solomon Ibn Gabirol

Good manners is thoughtfulness of God and man.

Sefer Maalot Ha-Middot

Do not interrupt while another speaks.

Sifre

Marriage

A woman of valor — who can find her? Her worth is far above rubies.

Bible

A man should always be careful to treat his wife with respect for it is only for the wife's sake that a man's house is blessed.

Shulhan Aruch

It is not good that man should live alone: I will make for him a helpmate.

Bible

I am my beloved's and my beloved is mine.

Bible

Patriotism

Seek the peace of the country where I have carried you and pray unto the Lord for it, for in its peace shall you have peace.

Bible

The law of the country is the law (to be observed by Jews).

Talmud

He who occupies himself with the affairs of the community is as one who studies Torah.

Talmud

When you have entered a city, abide by its customs.

Midrash

Peace

They shall beat their swords into plowshares and their spears into pruning hooks . . . Nation shall not lift up sword against nation, neither shall they learn war any more.

Bible

Beloved is peace. All blessings end with the blessings of peace.

Midrash

Great is peace! God created no finer virtue.

Midrash

Wherever there is justice there is peace and wherever there is peace there is justice.

Bible

Pity

He that is gracious to the humble, happy is he.

Bible

God feels pain each time that man suffers.

Mishnah

If your enemy is hungry, give him bread to eat and if he is thirsty, give him water to drink.

Bible

Do not hurt a hungry heart and do not anger a man who is in want.

Ben Sira

Prayer

O Lord, open Thou my lips and my mouth shall declare Thy praise.

Bible

Whoever has it in his power to pray on behalf of his neighbor and fails to do so is called a sinner.

Talmud

One should always first declare the praise of the Holy One, blessed be He, and then pray to Him.

Talmud

It is a good thing to give thanks unto the Lord and to sing praises unto His name.

Bible

Repentance

One must not say to a man who has repented (and changed his way of life): remember your former deeds.

Talmud

What is perfect repentance? It is when an opportunity presents itself for repeating an offense once committed and the offender, while able to commit the offense, nevertheless refrains from doing so because he is penitent and not out of fear or failure of vigor.

Maimonides

A twinge of conscience in a man's heart is better than all the flogging he may receive.

Talmud

Amend your ways and your doings.

Bible

Righteousness

The work of righteousness shall be peace.

Bible

To become righteous entails only the resolve to do good and love God.

Midrash

I have not seen the righteous forsaken.

Bible

This world would have been created even for one righteous man.

Talmud

Synagogue

My house shall be a house of prayer for all peoples.

Bible

Wherever ten Jews are found they are duty-bound to organize a synagogue. Moreover, whoever lives in a place where there is a synagogue and fails to join it is not a good neighbor.

Talmud

Enter unto His gates with thanksgiving and into His courts with praise.

Bible

I shall dwell in the House of the Lord forever.

Bible

Torah

Blessed be He who, in His Holiness, gave the Torah to His people Israel.

Siddur

When God gave the Torah on Mount Sinai there came down from heaven a book and a sword, and a heavenly voice said: "Choose one. If you choose the book, life will be yours; if you choose the sword, death must be yours."

Midrash

Our religion is a religion only by virtue of its Torah.

Emunot Ve-Deot

Would that they (the Jews) would forget Me (God) but keep My Torah.

Midrash

Truth

All His works are truth and all
His ways justice.

Bible

By three things is the world preserved: by truth, by law and order, and by peace.

Pirke Avot

This is the penalty for the liar: even when he tells the truth, no one believes him.

Talmud

The slanderer destroys himself, his victim and him who listens.

Talmud

Wisdom

Wisdom is better than rubies.

Bible

The Lord by wisdom founded the earth; by understanding he established the heavens.

Bible

Who is wise? He who learns from all men.

Pirke Avot

The final goal of wisdom is to turn to God and to do good works.

Talmud

Sabbath

God blessed the seventh day and made it holy.

Bible

The Sabbath is a queen whose coming changes the humblest home into a palace.

Talmud

You shall call the Sabbath a delight.

Bible

To plan for a mitzvah or for charity is permitted on the Sabbath.

Talmud

Rosh Hashanah

In the seventh month on the first day of the month you shall have a holy convocation; you shall not perform any servile work; it shall be a day of the sounding of the Shofar.

Bible

Rosh Hashanah is the birthday of the world.

Talmud

When a man sins during the year a record of his transgression is inscribed in faint ink. If he repents during the ten days of penitence the record is erased. If not, it is rewritten in indelible ink.

Midrash

All are judged on Rosh Hashanah.

Talmud

Yom Kippur

The purpose and aim of all creation is atonement.

Midrash

For transgressions against God Yom Kippur provides atonement; for offenses against fellow-men, the Day of Atonement does not provide atonement until man seeks the pardon of those he offended.

Mishnah

Who is the penitent man? Rabbi Judah said: The man who refrains from sinning even though the same opportunity to sin occurs more than once.

Mishnah

In the beginning sin is like a thread of a spider's web, but in the end it becomes like the cable of a ship.

Midrash

Sukkoth

You shall dwell in booths seven days.

Bible

Rejoice in your Festival and be altogether happy.

Bible

The Sukkah is a symbol of the Clouds of Glory in which the Almighty shielded the Israelites during their journey in the wilderness.

Talmud

The palm branch is like the spine; the myrtle is like the eye; the willow is like the mouth; and the ethrog is like the heart. With all thy limbs praise God.

Midrash

Hanukkah

All who are zealous for the Law
come out after me.

Book of Maccabees

Many candles can be kindled from one candle without diminishing it.

Midrash

Holy Lord of All Consecration, keep undefiled forever this house that has been so lately purified.

Book of Maccabees

Charity should be liberally dispensed on Hanukkah.

Shulhan Aruch

Purim

These days of Purim shall not fade among the Jews, nor their remembrance from their descendants.

Megillat Esther

Make them days of feasting and gladness and of sending portions to one another and gifts unto the poor.

Megillat Esther

How can I endure to see the evil that threatens my people?

Megillat Esther

On Purim we should be so gay that we cannot catch the distinction between "Down with Haman" and "Up with Mordecai."

Talmud

Passover

Passover — the season of our freedom.

Bible

Let all who are hungry enter and eat.

The Haggadah

You shall observe the Feast of unleavened bread.

Bible

In every generation every man must think of himself as having gone forth from Egypt.

The Haggadah

Shavuoth

You shall keep the Feast of Weeks (Shavuoth) unto the Lord your God.

Bible

Shavuoth recalls the day when all Israel was as one heart in accepting the Torah.

Zohar

The Torah was given publicly (on Shavuoth) in the wilderness, in no man's land, so that Jews may not say to others: you have no share in it.

Midrash

Like water, the Torah (given on Shavuoth) cleanses and is priceless and free.

Sifre